MILLION DOLLAR

NFT

EXPOSED TO NOVICE

COMPLETE BEGINERS GUIDE TO CREATE, INVEST AND SELLING OF NFT

BY

LARRY KIND

Table of Contents

INTRODUCTION

The term non fungible token (NFT) typically alludes to a cryptographic resource on the blockchain that addresses an immaterial and extraordinary computerized thing like a piece of craftsmanship, a photograph, an in-game collectible, or a tweet that various assets can't supersede because it has a lot of remarkable properties. Each NFT is novel and restricted in amount and not compatible; it can work as confirmation of legitimacy and proprietorship.

NFTs are recognized from each other by metadata and exceptional identifiers like a standardized tag. Metadata is known to be the information that makes up the data. Metadata permits clients to trade objects in light of their metadata rather than the whole article.

BASIC DETAILS OF NFT

NFTs mean to duplicate unmistakable properties of actual things like uniqueness, shortage and confirmation of proprietorship. Then again, fungible products can be traded on the grounds that their value, not one of a kind element, describes them. In any case, computerized items are just substantial when utilized related to their item.

The models of NFTs were hued coins, which allude to trial resources made on the Bitcoin network in 2012. The primary resource addressing a non fungible tradable blockchain marker was made in 2014 as an investigation for the Seven on Seven meeting at the New Museum in New York City.

While advanced collectibles and workmanship NFTs keep on drawing in the most consideration in the crypto local area, their potential use cases keep on expanding. They extend from the overall use cases like computerized craftsmanship and games to form, music, the scholarly community, tokenization of certifiable items, licenses, enrolment deals and dedication programs. There is additionally space for joining the upsides of NFT innovation with the usefulness of decentralized money

(DeFi). For instance, it is feasible to get and loan non fungible tokens, and they can be utilized as insurance to get an advance.

Anybody keen on selling and sharing their advanced manifestations like substance, workmanship, music and photography can make NFTs. Here is a down to earth guide on effectively getting on board with that fleeting trend of making a non fungible token.

NFT creation is a seriously straightforward cycle. For instance, clients can pick their substance and get a crypto wallet. They can pick an authentic NFT business focus and comply with its rules. After a NFT is made, it is fit to be sent off partners or proposed to specialists.

THIS IS WHAT YOU REALLY WANT TO FIND OUT ABOUT THE NFT CREATION PROCESS.

Understanding Nfts

One NFT gatherer paid $69.3 million for the computerized craftsmanship named "Everydays: The First 5000 Days" by Mike Winkelmann, otherwise called Beeple, making this NFT the costliest in the historical backdrop of crypto workmanship. The CryptoPunks assortment comprises of 10,000 pixelated pictures of troublemakers with a bunch of novel qualities, which spearheaded in 2015 on the Ethereum blockchain, sells for great many dollars.

The inquiry emerges: What is the worth of these computerized manifestations and for what reason are gatherers burning through such a lot of cash on them?

Beeple's "Everyday" a collection of 5,000 drawings referring to each day for the beyond thirteen-and-a-half years, was a laborious undertaking. Nonetheless, numerous NFT assortments, which are unquestionably fruitful, in all likelihood don't need an especially perplexing commitment from the creator.

Hence, for any individual who needs to turn into a NFT craftsman, it is fairly important to have an objective as a primary concern and an extraordinary degree of imagination. Regardless, for individuals who are not exactly so exceptionally gifted as Leonardo da Vinci anyway have a great deal of contemplations, making a NFT is beyond question worth troublesome. Likewise, for skilled workers by occupation who presumably at this point have a couple of Beeple-like expressive arts that are latent in the high level studio and essentially standing fit to be sold as NFTs, this could be a unimaginable feature start.

Honestly, an obscure individual's imaginative and engaging computerized craftsmanship piece won't arrive at the level of a frenzy as VIPs' manifestations like Canadian Singer Grimes' 10 advanced compositions which have been sold for about $6 million, NFT lets out of Kings of Leon which has made $2 million in bargains, or a captivating NFT which projected Jack Dorsey's first tweet, which sold for over $3 million.

All things considered, NFT innovation is great for protecting shortage and laying out responsibility for and substantial resources. It offers computerized makers strong choices for adapting their work and a degree of adaptability that is regularly ailing in the customary innovative industry's models. Connecting computerized content to the blockchain as a non fungible token is a protected and unquestionable method for selling it on the web. In addition, NFT creation offers specialists boundless induction to an overall association of specialists and comparable people.

Luckily, the most common way of making a NFT is neither expensive, complex nor specialized. Without composing any codes and with the right aide, anybody can make a NFT.

PICK THE ORGANIZATION AND PICK YOUR SUBSTANCE

First and foremost, makers need to pick the configuration of their NFT. They can create a non fungible token from any sight and sound document. It tends to be an advanced painting, a photograph, a text, a sound record, or a video from some eminent occasion. There are other inventive items, for example, crypto-collectibles, computer games' virtual things like symbols, weapons and cash, as well as virtual land in metaverses that can likewise be addressed as NFTs.

Obviously, there is space for makers' thoughts here, as it seems like all that advanced could be a NFT nowadays. For instance, it very well may be the World Wide Web's source code, which was sold by its innovator, Sir Tim Berners-Lee, as NFT for $5.4 million, a "high-res creative depiction" of educator George Church's genetic data, or the data of the essential person to anytime gathering their own DNA. Likewise, there is at this point a spot for non-progressed tokenized authentic assets, from land

and valuable stones to originator sneakers, all of which sell as NFTs..

With respect to the arrangement, makers are given finished opportunity of decision. It might rely upon the topic of their work of art and their creative mind.

Remember that after makers conclude what content and in which design they need to address as a NFT, they should change it over to a fitting document type, particularly on the off chance that it isn't as of now advanced. Most things will more often than not be put away as versatile organization designs (PNG) or illustrations trade design (GIF) records. Texts would commonly be accessible in compact report design (PDF), while music would probably be put away as MP3 and video kept as MP4.

STEP BY STEP INSTRUCTIONS TO MAKE AND MINT NFTS

The value of NFTs is based on their uniqueness. There are circumstances where clients should make a few indistinguishable duplicates of their manifestations. For instance, assuming that you sell a collectible, you may offer various variants, some more elite than others. For this situation, you really want to conclude the number of indistinguishable duplicates of a specific NFT you will incorporate inside the blockchain on the grounds that this number will be fixed and your NFTs become insusceptible to any alterations after their creation.

The most common way of making a non fungible token is called stamping. The term alludes to the most common way of transforming a computerized thing into a resource on the blockchain. Like how metal coins are made and added into dissemination, NFTs are printed whenever they are made. After the interaction, the advanced thing becomes sealed, safer and hard to control. Since it is addressed as a non fungible token, it can then be bought and exchanged, as well as carefully followed when it is exchanged or gathered again later on.

Some NFT advancements permit nonstop commissions to be paid to the first maker at whatever point a referred to thing changes proprietors. While printing a token, makers can program an eminence provision with the goal that resulting deals of their computerized thing create automated revenue for them. Assuming their work gets well known and expansions in esteem, they can receive financial advantage in return.

STEPS OF PRINTING AN NFT

The printing system starts when you've marked your NFT and paid the gas expense. You'll have the option to see your shiny new NFT on your profile after the exchange has been approved.

Pick the NFT commercial centre

After the computerized thing for a future NFT is prepared, the time has come to pick a NFT commercial centre to sell it.

Picking a stage is a fundamental piece of the most common way of printing NFTs, and the best decision here relies upon different elements including certain blockchain types, upheld guidelines and configurations, openness and a cost to mint a NFT.

The essential standard for tending to non-fungible modernized assets on the Ethereum blockchain was ERC-721. The ERC-1155 standard now offers semi-fungibility. Dissimilar to ERC-721, where the exceptional identifier addresses one resource, the remarkable identifier of the ERC-1155 token addresses an entire class of fungible resources, quite a few which the client can move to other people. Parts in light of the ERC-998 standard are the formats as indicated by which NFTs can be either non fungible or fungible resources.

Ethereum doesn't have a syndication on NFTs. In any case, most of the stages are Ethereum-based. Other non-Ethereum NFT commercial centers have a place with biological systems of blockchains like Cosmos, Polkadot, or Binance Smart Chain, to give some examples.

Every one of the NFT commercial centres works somewhat diversely and has its particular directions, as well as advantages and disadvantages. For instance, a portion of the NFTs are arranged while others are self-administration based. Making NFTs on certain stages is less expensive than others, while certain commercial centres don't uphold explicit document designs. A few stages are easy to use, while others have an intricate (UI) that could scare new clients.

Right now, there are a lot of NFT commercial centres in the crypto space. Non-organized stages have arisen as a suitable option to arranged ones since they give free admittance to all. To transfer NFTs onto them, clients just need to enlist and pay the exchange expense to mint a token.

One non-arranged stage is OpenSea that permits clients to mint and exchange NFTs, view information on them and really look at insights. Made in 2017, OpenSea keeps practically all crypto craftsmanship assortments, as well as countless things from numerous famous blockchain games. The stage has a reasonably easy to use creation interface that permits clients to rapidly and proficiently make a non fungible token free of charge.

Another mass commercial centre is Rarible, a self-administration stage that turns out to be interconnected with OpenSea. The method involved with making a NFT on Rarible is basically the same as OpenSea, however its usefulness is marginally unique. For instance, the quantity of configurations is restricted and the size of the works of art is more modest. By the by, Rarible has incredible traffic and permits clients to mint tokens prior to selling them, though OpenSea handles printing a symbolic when sold.

In contrast to self-administration stages, arranged ones are more particular with regards to makers. To begin selling the computerized content on SuperRare or Nifty Gateway, makers need to present an application structure with rigid determination models and a long sitting tight period for the specialists' choice.

Have a wallet setup for yourself with some cryptocurrency in it

A digital money wallet is a basic part of any blockchain framework. As indicated by the fundamental blockchain standards, clients need wallets to get to various stages, sign exchanges and deal with their equilibriums. Henceforth, NFT commercial centres dispense with the need to store client account information, making the stage safer.

A few cryptographic money wallet applications are accessible on cell phones to purchase and store digital currencies. Many are planned explicitly for blockchain newbies and can direct them through exchange charges, security and protection.

There are a ton of crypto wallets and program extensions for getting to blockchain-based applications that can put everything in order. Some arrangement extended security past a fundamental email address and mystery key with a twelve-word access. Prior to setting up a wallet, the main thing is to ensure that it matches the cryptographic money utilized on the stage you mean to utilize.

While hoping to mint a token on the blockchain, clients are expected to pay a gas charge. A gas expense alludes to an installment made by the client to make up for the figuring energy expected to process and approve exchanges on the blockchain. A gas limit is the most extreme measure of gas that a client will spend on a specific exchange.

Gas charges vacillate altogether relying upon the degree of interest for making exchanges. Stamping a NFT can be free. Nonetheless, it could cost between $10 to $100, contingent upon the picked commercial centre. (All things considered) on ends of the week when less individuals are executing, which will assist NFT fans with minimizing expenses assuming they are printing various things.

Stamping numerous things contrasts from twofold printing which alludes to stamping a similar NFT two times. Clients are not confined to take a similar computerized thing previously printed on one NFT commercial centre to an alternate one, stamping it a subsequent time and selling it again as another NFT. Clients need to remember all expected outcomes to their standing, for example, cheapening the predefined NFT and any ensuing advanced thing the client might need to sell, as the client's believability could be subverted. Hence, twofold printing ought to be tried not to by embed an imperceptible code into a computerized thing's document without essentially influencing the thing's appearance to the unaided eye.

Then, at that point, clients can download the digital currency wallet application to both their cell phones and PCs to get to NFT deals receipts, since they should have a method for getting crypto and convert it into customary cash at whatever point they need.

There are two primary ways of changing cryptographic money over to cash and in the end move it to a financial balance. To start with, you can utilize outsiders like crypto trades, ATMs and check cards. The subsequent choice is to utilize a distributed (P2P) stage. The two techniques are basic and safe. In any case, utilizing a shared exchange will in general be a speedier and more unknown method for trading your crypto for cash at a foreordained rate.

ADHERE TO THE NFT STAGE'S GUIDELINES

Each NFT commercial centre has explicit guidelines makers should continue to make a non fungible token.

Initially, the commercial centre normally requests that clients transfer a document they need to transform into a NFT with a title and a short depiction. Preferably, the NFT stage's clients need to invest some energy filling in their non fungible tokens' subtleties and idealizing them to draw in gatherers and expand the possibilities selling their manifestations. Subsequent to transferring the advanced thing, they will likewise have to pick whether to mint a solitary token or an assortment.

Besides, there are two potential choices for selling NFTs: fixed cost or sale. A decent value deal is the place where clients determine a cost at which they need to sell the NFT. It is really straightforward and direct. Barters are one more intriguing method for selling NFT manifestations. There are generally two kinds of closeouts accessible on various NFT commercial centres. The main sort is an English closeout, which is an expanding value sell off and the most noteworthy bid succeeds toward the end. There is additionally a type of English closeout considered coordinated sale when each parcel can be offered over a

[21]

characterized period and toward the finish of the period, the gatherer who has presented the most noteworthy offered successes and purchases a NFT. The subsequent kind is a Dutch sale, otherwise called diminishing value sell off, in which the value drops until somebody purchases a NFT.

APPROACHES TO SELLING A NFT

Then, at that point, contingent upon the commercial centre picked by the clients, they should set an underlying cost for their NFT. A few commercial centres likewise request to set an eminence rate, which is the sum clients will get when future gatherers sell their NFT. Setting a rate is a difficult exercise since a higher rate will get you more cash-flow per deal, yet it will likewise hinder individuals from exchanging your specialty in any case as they will be more averse to create a gain for themselves.

Additionally, there will be a choice to add record properties like an ideal goal and size. At last, the stage confirms the token and whenever supported, it is prepared available to be purchased.

Advancing The Nfts

With everything said and done, clients can decide to effectively advance their newly printed NFT creation. The advancement of a NFT will rely upon a client's NFT particulars. In any case, there are a few nuts and bolts makers can focus on like understanding the purchaser or viable formation of an advancement technique.

Perhaps the most proficient advancement procedure is advertising, which alludes to fostering a positive standing inside the local area by sharing great data about you and your NFT assortment.

Likewise, it very well may be advanced by internet publicizing, remembering distributions for specialty papers and appearances on crypto webcasts, as well as web-based media advancement.

CONCLUSION

On the off chance that makers are searching for the greatest gatherers, it would check out to engage the biggest crowd conceivable, and utilizing web-based media could go far since clients can share the connections to their advanced things across their and the NFT commercial centre's web-based media. Twitter, Telegram and Discord have as of now settled correspondence stations for the crypto local area, where clients can make individual records on them to advance their NFTs, lay out a standing and work on broad mindfulness. Therefore, they can meet a few powerhouses and craftsmen to work together with or columnists of well-known outlets who will expound on themselves and their NFT assortment.

For NFT makers, growing a steadfast local area could be indispensable for the advancement since these individuals will continually uphold them, spread the word about them, put resources into them and eagerly purchase their N FT manifestations.

Printed in Great Britain
by Amazon